FREE
THYSELF

CAMELIA A. STRAUGHN

FREE THYSELF

WORDS OF LOVE, PAIN AND VICTORY

Rising STAR

Rising STAR Publishing
www.risingstarlifecoach.com

Copyright © 2016 by Camelia Straughn. All rights reserved. No part of this book may be used or reproduced in any manner whatsoever without the written permission of the author. The only exceptions are brief quotations embodied in critical articles or reviews.

Special discounts on bulk quantities of Rising STAR Publishing books are available. For details, contact Rising STAR at info@risingstarlifecoach.com.
To contact the author, email risingstarlifecoach@gmail.com

ISBN: 978-0-9973607-0-7

First Edition
(March 2016)

Printed in the United States

Rising STAR Publishing
www.risingstarlifecoach.com

Contents

Publisher's Note i
Dedication.. iii
Letter from the Author.. ¡Error! Bookmark not defined.

Words of Love, Pain and Victory

1. Who Will.. 1
2. Changed Love 4
3. Damn! Another free ass whoopin 6
4. Her Eyes 9
5. Strong Woman 11
6. Finally.. 13
7. Looking for Love 14
8. Long Ago 15
9. Reflection 17
10. Giving Up.. 19
11. Sister, Queens.. 20
12. Remember 22
13. 901 4th Street 23
14. Case Number 24
15. Full Circle.. 25
16. Touch My Soul.. 27
17. Cries of A Counselor... 28
18. A Mother's Prayer 29
19. Passion... 31
20. Answer Me 33
21. Look.. 35
22. Peace 36
23. Sunshine 38
24. Tracey 39
25. A Salute to Diane 42
26. Zachary.. 45

27. Kiss Me 47
28. I Attract that which I Am 49
29. When We First Made Love 50
30. His Rib 52

Publisher's Note

This publication was created to share the journey of the writer and to show that no matter what if one persists victory is yours.

This will be the first of many publications brought to via Rising STAR. It is our hope that you will find value and sustenance via the words of our authors.

We pray to the Creator of us all that our intentions are clear and pure and that we may be of service to the Creator's will.

Dedication

I dedicate this work to the DIVINE CREATOR, Father Mother God, who always knows exactly what I need, exactly when I need it. And for whom I could not live and breathe.

Finally, to my King, my Children and other Family and Friends. You have allowed me to create a life of peace, love and joy. For that I will be forever grateful! Loving you all with all the love in my heart, Always! I send you Peace, Love and Light.

A LETTER TO MY READERS

Peace and blessings Beautiful Ones.

Life is wonderful, beautiful even. It is a continuously unfolding story, a story that is unique to you as is mine.

If you are reading this letter it means you have made the decision to enter my world, for that I thank you, and I am grateful that you have decided to purchase my book.

It is my hope that as you read my poetry that you can see me and at times even relate to my journey. Knowing that we are all one and we are all connected. Also, when you are done, I pray that you are uplifted and inspired. Knowing that life is a journey not a destination, and that you will be moved to enjoy your journey and embrace every trial and lesson. Loving you with all the love in my heart.

                              Peace, Love and Light
                              Camelia

FREE THYSELF

WORDS OF LOVE, PAIN AND VICTORY

CAMELIA A. STRAUGHN

WHO WILL

She came to me broken and defeated.
The journey of life has beat the fight out of her.
Her heart broken and eyes filled with tears, begging and pleading for relief!
Who will hold her, listen to her, who has been through what she has been through?
The source of love, peace, help and encouragement to those around her.
Administering words of healing and hope.
Yet, now she stands alone...lifeless and wishing that it all would end.
No longer asking it to stop....but, wanting it all to end.
Who will hold her, listen to her, who has been through what she has been through?
Wanting to pull herself up, refusing to be a

victim, yet not having the strength to hold herself up.

Wounded, broken, screaming through her smile for help and no one sees her pain nor do they hear her cry's.

Who will hold her, listen to her, who has been through what she has been through?

She has been the source of love, peace, help and hope to all who share her space.

When will someone see into her eyes and see her pain, the need to be lifted up as she lifted those in her world.

Who will be the wind beneath her wings.

Who will allow her to cry, allowing her soul to be cleansed without judgment?

No longer asking it to stop....but, wanting it all to end.

The journey of life has beat the fight out of her.

Who will hold her, listen to her, love her, who

has been through what she has been through?
No one notices the pain through her smile. For it lights up every room she enters.
No longer asking it to stop...But, wanting it all to end.
Screaming someone pray for me...and no one hears her cry through her smile.
Who will hold her, listen to her, who has been through what she has been through?
Now there is silence, for when she cried no one noticed for she was the source of love, peace, help, hope and encouragement for all those who came in contact with her. Now! No longer asking it to stop...wanting it all to end.

Changed Love

I remember when we first met, I was the most important thing to you. Daily you would touch me, talk to me, hold me, and assure me that you and I would always be. Now... it seems as if I am no longer important to you. I share my thoughts, my feelings, my wanting to be close to you and you say that I'm starting a fight. So now, sharing my feeling and my thoughts of the position that we are in is no longer allowed, no longer respected, no longer wanted and no longer recommended. How did we get here? How did this happen? I feel confused lost and lonely, not only because of the distance but more because of the lack of communication, the lack of understanding, the lack of wanting and the lack of allowing me to make things clear. Who have we become? what have we become, so that you will easily recommend that I go my own way, if that is what I want to do. Someone once said that if your mate tells you that it's okay for you to leave that it's probably best that you should leave because holding on is not going to be healthy. Holding on to a person who no longer wants to hold on to you is devastating to the mind, spirit the soul and the concept of love itself. Look at me, my tears are real they flow uncontrollably and I no longer feel that this is Cleansing, because the hurt runs deep, deeper than I care to explain. How did we get here? What happened? I ask myself did I do something to cause our love to dry up as if it never had life or is it just time, are you that one who was to just be in my life for a season when my mind and my heart is wanting you to be here for a lifetime.

Damn! another free ass whoopin

(SCREAMING) - Damn another free ass whooping I'm giving

What did I do now I cannot seem to remember? I'm trying to stay alive another day. damn another free as whopping given

Ok, wait, what is today? It's Friday... time to heal before Monday... damn another free ass whooping.... Screaming and begging, wait please! The kids can see you. Through bloody mouth and swollen eyes, no baby I'm okay.... Daddy didn't mean to hurt me, I am fine.

No please not tonight this is going to make it harder to cover, what did I do wrong this time? I'm sorry!

Damn! Another free ass whooping I'm giving. Oh my, It's Saturday, does he not see what he's doing to me; wait did I do something wrong maybe? I should be more understanding. Maybe I should try to love him more, it's Sunday, see he didn't mean it, these flowers are beautiful! He tells me he loves me. I smile, and tell myself he loves me, he is sorry he didn't mean it.

It's Monday the swelling has gone down yeah! I can use my concealer and foundation and no one will know... another free ass whoopin I have given. Tuesday Wednesday Thursday Friday life is good he loves me... Wait!! what's that noise..? wait! NO what's wrong? you promised you said it would never happen again. What did I do wrong? Damn! another free ass whoopin I am giving, given, gave! do not yell, do not cry, the kids are close by.

I can't move, wait, where are they taking me? Something is wrong, I'm standing here can you hear me why is there blood coming from my head, from my face? Do you not see me standing here? Where are they taking me? Hey I'm right here! Damn another free ass whoopin I have given......and today it took my life.

HER EYES

Look into her eyes, what can you see?
Promise, hope, and love.
Her skin is a deep, dark, flawless brown.
Her smile is so bright it will save a million
Souls. When she walks into a room, her
presence consumes it. As she moves across
the floor, every man wants to know her and
every woman envies her.
No, look again, look into her eyes....
deep...yes, deep into her eyes. See the little girl
fighting to get out, yelling help me! Can anyone
see me? Can someone save me? Can you, no
you, yes you? Can you see what he did to me?
Can you see what he did to me? Can you tell
why mother never believed me?

Look into her eyes, she cries.... Help me, save me! Can anyone see me! Can anyone hear me!

He took my soul, my prize and my innocence.... how do I get it back? Can someone save me? Can anyone hear me? Can anyone see me?

Yet, now.... I walk across the room and man wants to know me and every woman envies me.

Eyes full of confidence, skin a deep, dark, flawless brown, and a smile that will heal a million Souls, yet...she carries a heart that is forever broken.

Look into her eyes, what DO you see?

STRONG WOMAN

They say I am strong, Should I believe
They say I can make it should I try
Strong woman am I, Strong woman I must be
I can bring a smile to anyone's face, just through my smile, helping them see the sunshine in their own eyes.
The words I speak to others help them realize their dreams, the impossible becomes, I'm Possible!
Strong woman am I, Strong woman I must be
See my man left me the other night, alone with no clue of what to do. I have a male child you see, and now it's all up to me to teach him how to be a man. Everything he will learn, comes

from a woman in pain. How could this be, this is not what we agreed on.

Strong woman am I, strong woman I must be I cried and cried and cried...there was no one there to dry my eyes.

Strong woman I am, strong woman I must be Who created this concept...Strong woman..., to where I am left without, left alone...?

Strong woman I am; strong woman I must be. I fight and scream in hopes that someone will realize that this weight is heavy on me. They say I am strong; they say I can make it. Should I believe, should I try!

Strong woman am I, strong woman I must be Strong woman yes! That's Me....

Finally

As I sit here and close my eyes I think,
"Finally, peace."
Clear, free of all the demons that your love
passed on to me.
Letting go of the low self-esteem.
Believing in the Creator and me.
Giving my children a new sense of love and life.
Believing that the Creator is in control.
Not allowing you to control.
Finally, a woman coming out, out of pain and
abuse.
Finally letting go of the pain knowing that the
Creator will work it all out just for me.
Finally loving me, my own self.
Finally!

Looking for Love

Looking for love in all the wrong places.
Sharing my dreams with all the wrong faces.
Praying to the Creator for a mate,
who would be true.
Then along came you.
A kiss so sweet and tender. A touch gentle,
yet strong.
Arms that gave me security where there was
none.
A hug that seemed to last forever.
Finally, a love that will last my whole life through.
Sharing my dreams with you, is my dream come
true.
Because you love me, and I love you.

Long Ago

So long ago, I believed that you were all I needed.
Then, for some reason, you turned your back on me.
You stopped loving me, but refused to let me go.
Continued to hurt, but refused to let me go.
I remember all the nights I cried and begged you to love me
and yet,
you continued to refused, but you refused to let me go.
I always believed you don't hurt the one you love.
You made the other woman more important than us.
You promised to be a father to our daughter,

yet you let her down before her life could begin.
You promised to be a father to my son, yet you let him down with no real man to believe in.
So long ago I believed that you were all I needed,
but now I know that I don't need you at all.
Sad to say that thought still hurts.
Yet I know that the day will come when God will send Mr. Right for me to me.
No more tears, no more fears.
No more pain.
No more heartache.
So long ago.

REFLECTION....... I sit and I
reflect back on my life and read the words I have

written

over the years

and how I somehow believed that I had found

true love.

Not really looking at the whole picture.

Believing false promises.

I sit and listen to Gerald Levart's CD play and
I finally believe the Creator has sent my Mr.

Right for me.

My Mr. too damn good to me.

I believe I have finally have been given a love

that can be true.

You have allowed me to really open up.

When I close my eyes, I see you and have no

regrets.

I can feel your strong, but gentle touch.

In such a short time you have shown me that

love
should not be hard nor
should it hurt.
You are everything I need, everything I've wanted.
A man pure in heart and soul.
Someone I can truly believe in.
I pray to Allah that this love will never end.
I have finally been blessed with a good thing.
Someone who knows that he has found a great thing.
Someone who will cherish and love me.
I have been given a chance to open up and allow love to take over me.
Every second we are apart I long to be by your side.
No longer do I need to reflect on the past.
Just more forward with the love the Creator has given me

Giving Up

Giving up to save my heart.
Too much pain, to many bad memories.
Giving up to give peace to my soul.
Too much lost and nothing gained.
Giving up to save myself from rejection.
Too many times have t given my love and paid
for everyone's mistakes.
Giving up wanting only to love and be loved.
That I have realized I will never find.
Giving up because I must let go.
Remembering how much I loved you and
realizing
that you don't love me.
Only pain and hate in my heart.

Sisters, Queens

Africa in Your Eyes

Look around at my sisters

I see Africa in your eyes

Your walk is amazing

And no one can copy

My sisters, African queens

We come in different shapes and sizes

But elegant we all are

I see Africa in your eyes

Hair natural and free

Styles that are designed

From the heart

I see Africa in your eyes

My sisters, African queens

Being real true to yourself

I see Africa in your eyes

Walking tall a strength unknown

Talking strong, a knowledge that comes

From years before

My sisters, African queens

I see Africa in your eyes

Remembering

I sit in my chair as I watch my children play,
feeling my third child move inside me, watching
my stomach grow with life.
Wondering what he'll be like,
praying to the Creator that I will be the mother
they all need me to be.
Realizing I must be both mother and father.
Knowing I will make this journey alone.
Only my children to love me.
Remembering to be grateful even though,
as a woman, I need more.
Wanting someone to love me and make me feel
special.
Sitting and watching my children play.
Remembering to be grateful.

901 4th Street

Help!
Can anyone hear me?
Help!
The world, my family has abandoned me.
How could I live in a world so cold?
How do I survive in a world that doesn't care?
How do I learn to love?
How do I learn to respect myself?
No one ever taught me what love is, or what respect means.
Help!
Can anyone hear me?

Case Number

Scream, scream.
That's all I do.
No other means of communication; loud, out of hand.
No other type of behavior.
Curse, curse.
I know no other words.
You judged me, but never get to know.
You condemn me, before you try to help me.
Can't you see my pain.
You have read about my hurt.
Can someone please believe in me?
Can someone please teach me?
Scream, curse, loud out of hand,
That's all I know.

Full Circle

Coming full circle
So much pain, one day I will write of joy and real love.
Coming full circle,
that you are no longer part of me. Learning to let go.
My heart shattered into pieces and my mind clouded of what is true.
Coming full circle,
you no longer love me. Having to accept that the time has come.
Caring life, knowing I must do this alone.
Realizing everything is not as it seems.
Coming full circle,
how can I continue to believe?
My heart shattered into pieces, my mind racing, not knowing what is true.

Coming full circle,
realizing my love, you have tossed away.
Coming full circle, doing it all alone.

Touch My Soul

Someone touch my soul.
Someone to believe in me. Help me reach my dreams.
Feeling me always.
Someone to touch my soul, that inner most part of me that only the right person can reach.
Feel my heart and my love, without making love
Feel my pain without causing it.
Someone to touch my soul, will that day ever come?
Always reaching out and catching the wrong one.
Someone to touch my soul, that inner most part of me that only the right one can reach.
Believe in me, love me only forever.
Someone to touch my soul

Cries of A Counselor

They won't listen.
They won't follow directions.
How do I help?
Where do I make a difference?
How can I help?
No respect for the ones who care.
Why do I have to endure?
Why do I listen to their words?
They never know, how their words sting and how they hurt.
Not knowing, what they say.
They don't want to be helped.
They don't want to be loved.
God, help me, give me strength.
Don't let me give up, don't let me give in.
They won't listen.
They don't want to be helped.

A Mother's Prayer

May you enter this world with no problems.
May you grow to know Allah.
May he keep you safe.
In and out of the womb.
Always look to Allah to guide you.
Never fail to pray, never give up your faith.
Always believe that Allah is always around.
I leave this for you.
To remind you of my love for you.
Look to Allah for all your needs.
I pray that all these things you will hold dear.
I pray that you will always look to Allah for he is all you need.

Passion

Passion feels my body and soul when I look at you.
My mind becomes blank trying to keep up with the beat of my heart.
Passion- the heat that flows between us.
Electricity that lights up the room, my body becoming one with yours...
Forgetting the world and all that is in it.
Passion- closing my eyes and seeing us kiss and touch and feel passion.
Heat, sweat, joy
Feels my body and soul.
Feel me with your passion.
Touch me and make me hot.
Feel my passion and know that it will last.

Answer Me

A world of pain, can it stop?
Will it stop?
Dear God, help me change.
No hope, no love, no place to call my own.
Everyone has the answer; no one tries to really see my pain.
Do this, do that.
Can anyone really tell me, teach me?
Hell, show me how to love me, love you, love life.
No.
Yet, everyone has an answer
Wake up. Stop hurting yourself.
Why?
Can't you see this is all I know.
Can't you see this is what my world is? No.
Yet, everyone has an answer.
Answer to what?

Not my question, not my pain.
Listen to me, hear me- do you see?
All I have trusted; all I have believed has failed me- No
Yet, everyone has an answer.
Can you feel it? Can you see?
No love for me. No place to call my own.
Listen. No- listen, please
See my tears, they are real. Stop hurting yourself.
Why?
No answer given to me. No one believes in me.
Just demands.
Listen. Will you please listen.
Hear me. No
Yet, everyone has an answer.

Look

Look around, what do I see?
Much confusion, much pain.
No one knows where they're going.
No smiles, no sharing, no believing.
Giving nothing, taking all.
Self-serving.
How could this be? Can't we see the pain?
Am I the only one?
Can anyone hear, listen? Listen.
Shh
Look around what do I see?
A world doomed. Hate being the norm.
Hate thy brother.
Hate thy sister.
Listen, look around, what do I see?
Much confusion, much pain.
No smiles, no sharing, no believing.
Listen.
We must change.

PEACE

Peace comes as we get closer to the Divine
Peace is feeling of comfort and security that only the Divine can give.
I pray for peace, I long for peace
A peace that I know that only the Divine can give
Peace brings a level of light that no one can destroy
Pray for light, Pray for peace
Use your faith in the Divine that He/She will make it all alright
Knowing that He/She will give you Peace
Peace just for you, just for me
The Peace only the Divine can give
So, as I grow and make my connection with the Divine
I realize that the Peace was within me all the Time.

Sunshine

Sunshine kisses. A ray of hope.
I see
Sunshine comes from strange places, but can sunshine come from me?
Smile, give joy to all that you see.
Make this world a better place.
Sunshine in your eyes. A ray of hope.
I see.
Sunshine kisses. A ray of hope.
I see.
Quiet, gentle, strong. Sunshine kisses.
Touch me and feel the light, believe in sunshine kisses. A ray of hope.
Sunshine share them with me.

Tracey

So many things are temporary,
the trees, the flowers, the grass.
Nothing is here to stay.
Life has handed you many hard cards to play.
But now you're in a better place.
No longer tired, no longer alone.
No longer will you be disappointed.
No one will be able to lie to you again.
Everything is so temporary.
But now you are in a place that will never end.
Love, peace, is what you now have. Forever
more.
Life for us here must go on.
Our eyes are filled with tears, our hearts are
heavy and wrecked with pain.
But that too is temporary.
Comfort comes with the memory of who you

were and what you believe.
The smiles, the many times we spent
dancing and partying.
You know that they love you,
and that you loved us. Enjoy your peace.
Because this will not be temporary.

This poem was written for my youngest sister who passed long before we were ready for her to go! I miss you dearly....

A Salute to Diane

Oh how the trumpets sang when the Creator called you away.

my heart sank as I watched you pass away.

how strong you were to hold on until I could come.

I held your hand and sang to you letting you know that I loved you.

Remembering the years of heartache and pain.
now all that has passed away.
Yes, people will mourn,
but for you I will rejoice for life can no longer tried to steal your joy.
As I watched you take your last breath,
I could feel the peace that you had received
knowing that the Creator would watch over me
we all make plans,

But the Creator is the best of planners of this
I am sure.
Someone asked me do I feel because for you I have decided to be strong all I could say was yes almost as loud as I could. my mother is gone and I'm not quite sure why.
My children will no longer get to enjoy her smile, they will never get to experience Diane like so many of us did,
and she will no longer get to feel their hugs and kisses.
But I will tell them of her and make sure her memory lives on.
Mother I love you and I am not sad for we were able to mend the past.
So know that I love you I realize the Creator makes no mistakes and you are now forever in a better place.
Mommy I love you

Zachary

Zachary, when I first heard about you;
I longed and waited to be able to meet you.
That will not happen now because the Creator
had another plan.
He decided that he wanted you closer to him in
a place of eternal peace, love, and no physical
or emotional pain. You leave behind a mother a
father and hundreds of family and friends who
don't understand why your life had to end.
But I say the Divine knew you were too good
to be left down here.
He wanted you to be able to speak on their
behalf closely in his ear.
Although they will never get to hold your hand
again, and I will never get the chance,
I do believe that this was part of the Creator's
master plan.

You see we understand that you were a loan
from the Creator to us.
and now he's carried you to your eternal home,
where you can constantly remind him how great
we are.
Because the Creator adds an extra hedge of
protection when a child speaks for us.
Zachary, you will be missed and always loved.
We will try not to be selfish and try to rejoice,
because you are now in the best place that the
Creator created for us.

I Stand Firm

I will never fall, I will never break, I stand firm that's how strong my love is...
I feel the earth shake under my feet, yet I stand firm, that is how strong my love is...
My soul feels the energy and heat of your touch and my body is on fire.
The smell of you excites me and my body shakes with the anticipation of feeling your touch.
I stand firm, no matter the circumstance that is how strong my love is....
No length of time, no distance that comes between us will shake my Love. I stand firm.
I await your return longing to feel your lips glide across my body.
Recognizing and feeling the deepness of our closeness. My soul yearns for your touch.
I stand firm, that's how much I love you

Kiss Me

Kiss my hand and my wrist and my arm.
Feel the heat from my soul.
Watch my body come alive again.
Feel the heat from my soul.
I look into your eyes and I see a new beginning.
Kiss my face my lips and my neck.
Feel the heat from my soul.
Take my hand and we will rise and love together.
Watch my body come alive when our bodies become one.
Feel the heat from my soul.
I am free.
Feel the heat my soul.
You encourage me to love and you.

I trust you give me the courage to feel again.

Feel the heat from my soul.

and you I trust.

Kiss me on my stomach thigh and my life spot.

Feel the heat from my soul,

and you I trust.

Yes, it's you I trust.

I ATTRACT THAT WHICH I AM

I attract that which I am

I am Love

I am Honesty

I am Gratitude

I am Smart

I am Kind

I am Trustworthy

I am Peaceful

I am inspiration

I attract which I am

When We First Made Love

I have been touched by an angel.
I'm glad that you are part of my life.
When we made, love time stands still and all is
right with the world.
Going on long walks, holding hands and the
trees dance because of our love.
We are in example to all the world of what real
love looks like.
I have been touched by angel.
Loving you was what I was made to do.
I'm glad that you are part of my life.
I have never felt this way before I want to be
your everything.
I wish that we could go to a quiet place so that
we can make love,
making time stand still showing the world what
real love is.

I can't get enough of you

When you are away, I long to be close to you.
Our hearts beat to the say rhythm.
A real love is what we have.
I've been touched by an angel.
I love loving you, making time stand still.
Being together until the end of time, I will love you forever.
Without you, I do not want to live.
You were made especially for me.
I love you, I love you.
I've been touched by an angel.
Making love and time stands still.

HIS RIB

I am his Rib, protecting him and giving him balance

I am his Rib, strong with just enough curve to create a source of completion, making it possible for him to know rest and peace.

I am his Rib, to stand beside him and be his council, strong yet tender and sweet.

I am his Rib, speaking life and love into him, so he knows he is my King and as he long as he follows the Divine I will follow him.

I am his Rib, that inner strength that allows him to lead to be the head and not the tail.

I am his Rib, the beautiful source that holds him together.

ALSO FROM RISING STAR

BOOKS

Composition of a Soul's Journey (Camelia A. Straughn)

Women Intimacy and Religion Workbook (Camelia A. Straughn)

FORTHCOMING

Finding Your Bliss in the Midst of Pain: The 9 Keys to Trusting Yourself and Living and Extraordinary Life (Camelia Straughn)

Tales of a Florida Girl (Lakadar Davison)

www.risingstarlifecoach.com

www.ingramcontent.com/pod-product-compliance
Lightning Source LLC
Chambersburg PA
CBHW070106100426
42743CB00012B/2666